A view of the State House in Philadelphia as it was in 1799.

COVER: *A colonial officer rallies his men for the final, victorious charge against the French and their Indian allies in the Battle of Lake George on September 8, 1755— the first test of the yeomanry of the New World against the disciplined troops and the experienced officers of the Old. For another view of the battle, see pages 114–15.*

GLEN FALLS INSURANCE COMPANY

FRONT ENDSHEET: *New France's Governor Frontenac orders an Indian tortured.*

ONONDAGA HISTORICAL ASSOCIATION

CONTENTS PAGE: *A detail of a Dutch map depicts the 1650 image of America.*

STOKES COLLECTION, NEW YORK PUBLIC LIBRARY

BACK ENDSHEET: *The English assault at Freshwater Cove, near Louisbourg.*

MABEL BRADY GARVAN COLLECTION, YALE UNIVERSITY ART GALLERY

*"A knowledge of the past prepares us for the crisis
of the present and the challenge of the future."*

JOHN F. KENNEDY
From his special foreword in Volume 1

THE AMERICAN HERITAGE
NEW ILLUSTRATED HISTORY
OF THE UNITED STATES

VOLUME 2
COLONIAL AMERICA

By ROBERT G. ATHEARN
Professor of History, University of Colorado

CREATED AND DESIGNED BY THE EDITORS OF
AMERICAN HERITAGE
The Magazine of History

PUBLISHED BY
DELL PUBLISHING CO., INC., NEW YORK

CONTENTS OF THE COMPLETE SERIES

Foreword by JOHN F. KENNEDY
Introduction by ALLAN NEVINS
Main text by ROBERT G. ATHEARN

A MASTER INDEX FOR ALL 16 VOLUMES APPEARS IN VOLUME 16

CONTENTS OF VOLUME 2

CHAPTER 4

THE COLONIES GROW

From the seedlings that were Plymouth and Jamestown, English settlements spread out all along the Atlantic seacoast. While the Cape Cod region was somewhat less attractive than the more verdant land of Virginia, it was here that the first real population growth occurred. Hardly had the Pilgrims set up their village at Plymouth before their own promoter, Thomas Weston, sent out a group of rowdy individuals to settle nearby and establish a fishing post. Irresponsible, ignorant of the demands of a New England winter, the latest arrivals neglected to plant crops or make other necessary preparations. Their settlement was a failure.

Not far away another attempt floundered and finally came under the control of Thomas Morton, who rocked conservative New England to its foundations by turning his colony into the gayest settlement in America. Calling his place Merry Mount, he put up an enormous Maypole around which his men danced, drank, and

John Eliot was preacher to the Indians and translator of the Bible into their language. He was 55 when painted in 1659.

frolicked with the Indians and their women. As the natives approved, and brought their beaver skins to Merry Mount instead of Plymouth, the Pilgrims watched the continuous party with righteous indignation.

By 1628, there were several communities planted along the shores of Massachusetts Bay. A fishing post started in 1623 at Cape Ann, on the north rim, was unsuccessful, but those who refused to go home moved southward to found the town of Salem. The residents sent word to England that their little community would be a haven for those dissatisfied with the religious situation at home. They were answered by a Reverend John White of Dorchester, an Anglican minister who, although unhappy with the official church, did not want to separate in the manner of Pilgrims. He and his followers became known as Puritans, since they hoped merely to purify the church, not destroy it. By appealing to some London businessmen, who saw economic opportunity in America, White sparked the formation of the New England Company. It was given a charter in 1628, and at once sent out John Endecott as director.

One of his first official acts in America was to send Miles Standish across Massachusetts Bay to Merry Mount to chop down poor Morton's Maypole. Colonizing was supposed to be a serious business!

In 1629, the New England Company was rechartered under the name of the Massachusetts Bay Company. Like the Mayflower Compact, the new charter was to be significant in American history. Because of the insistence of Puritan squire John Winthrop, who wanted to sponsor a small emigration, there would be no governing council in England. The control of the colony would be in America. That condition satisfied, Winthrop was elected governor and organization proceeded. By the next spring the company was transferred to America. During that year 840 immigrants arrived in Massachusetts; it was the largest group yet to leave home. Significantly, the arrivals represented not only workers but some men of means who had qualities of leadership. Understandably, 1630 is called the year of the great migration —caused by discontent with Charles I, who ignored Parliament and was arbitrary in both political and religious matters. The Massachusetts Bay Colony was not without food shortages and personal suffering, but after the first few years, growth was rapid. By 1643, the population stood somewhere between 14,000 and 16,000, which was perhaps more than the entire population of England's other American colonies.

Colonies breed colonies

At a rather tender age the Massachusetts Bay Colony gave birth to a whole litter of small colonies. Within three or four years after Winthrop's arrival, outposts from both the Pil-

The four ships John Winthrop brought to New England (left) are anchored in Boston harbor, where his group settled after first landing at Salem, the colony governed by the Puritan John Endecott (above).

grims' settlement and those along the bay were established in the fertile Connecticut Valley, and America's great westward movement was launched.

Within a few years, after having allied to ward off the Pequot Indians, several towns along the valley joined to frame an agreement that called for self-government. Removed not only from England but the coastal settlements as well, these people found it necessary to take things into their own hands. The Fundamental Orders of Connecticut, while not particularly liberal, provided some political safeguards that marked a gain in the quest for a measure of local control.

New Hampshire and Maine were also offspring of Massachusetts. Lack of interest in them by their sponsors, coupled with the fact that the residents (who had come largely from Massachusetts) looked more and more to the older colony for guidance, spelled their failure as independent enterprises. In 1644, after a few struggling years, New Hampshire was taken over by the Bay Colony; a similar absorption of Maine took place 14 years later. Not until 1679 would New Hampshire again become a separate colony, and Maine would remain a part of Massachusetts until 1820, when it became a state in the Union.

More independent were the little settlements in Rhode Island. The leaders there were two dissidents named Roger Williams and Anne Hutchinson. Williams, one of the most original thinkers in America of his time, believed the church in Massachusetts was not separate enough from the Anglican church and that it meddled too much in politics. So loud was his complaint about this and such requirements as taxation to support religion and compulsory attendance that in 1635 he was banished from Massachusetts. He promptly established his followers at Providence, Rhode Island. He was joined by Mrs. Hutchinson, who, with her exiles, settled at a place later known as Portsmouth. Williams next went to London and got a charter for his colony, despite the bitter opposition of the Massachusetts Bay powers. Thus legitimatized, Rhode Island went forward in its development, and by insisting upon complete separation of church and state, carved another support for American democracy.

The rapid spread of the Connecticut frontier produced problems. Typically, the whites refused to recognize Indian claims, insisting that cultivation proved ownership, and before long there was violence. The settlers appealed to Boston for help, but the situation was so pressing that they were obliged to raise a force for their own defense. Volunteers, led by experienced Indian fighters, attacked the natives, and before the battle was over, 500 Pequots were burned alive or killed as they tried to flee. The rest were enslaved or sold in the West Indies. For the next 250 years, in succeeding Western settlements, the story would be the same.

Out of the bloody affair there arose the Confederation of New England —colonial settlements joined for mutual protection. Organized in 1643, the Confederation was a "firm and

Roger Williams, banished from Massachusetts in 1635 for his liberal views, is shown landing in Rhode Island in an 1858 painting by Alonzo Chappel.

perpetual league of friendship" and stands as the first attempt at a confederacy of colonies in North America. Aside from its defense duties, the league aimed to provide its members with such services as the return of runaway servants, escaped prisoners, and other law violators. Under some circumstances it even proposed to make treaties with foreign powers. Perhaps its founders were too optimistic; within 20 years the Confederation began to disintegrate. Aside from the bickering that took place, and the attempted dominance of Massachusetts, England itself frowned upon the league's efforts to engage in diplomatic relations with the French and Dutch over their colonies, which flanked New England. The conquest of New Netherland by the English in 1664 eased one of the major pressures that originally had inspired the union. Despite its transitory nature, however, the Confederation taught a lesson in the virtues of cooperation that would be remembered at a later and more critical time.

The lords go west

Not all the English colonies in America were managed by joint enterprise. Maryland, for example, owes its origin to George Calvert, the first Lord Baltimore, who in 1632 was granted a charter by the king. Calvert's older son Cecilius took over the grant upon his father's death and became the proprietor of a 10,000,000-acre feudal estate in the wilds of North America. All he owed the king were two Indian arrows a year and one-fifth of the gold and silver found upon the land. This was merely a recognition of the king as feudal superior, and as few or no precious metals were found, young Calvert could not complain about high taxes.

Cecilius Calvert, who now became Lord Baltimore, and his young brother Leonard managed their colony well. Although they were Catholics, they allowed extensive liberties to Protestants who wanted to settle. As businessmen, they were more interested in making a profit than in quarreling over religious beliefs. Thanks to such sound judgment, Maryland prospered from the beginning, and while there were no magnificent returns, there was also no starvation period. To show they were sincere in their desire for religious toleration, the Calverts caused to be passed in 1649 an Act Concerning Religion. The Puritan-controlled assembly did not produce an act as liberal as Lord Baltimore wished, but it provided an encouraging basis for future legislation.

Politically the colony followed a course of increasing liberality. For the first few years Leonard Calvert governed it personally, but in 1637, Cecilius, who had never come to Maryland, directed Leonard to call together the local council. At first the council had no power, but gradually it assumed some, and by 1642 it held that, like the English Parliament, it had the right to convene when it saw fit. By 1650, it had been divided into two houses, with a majority in both required for the passage of laws.

Socially there was less democracy. In the early period there were about 60 manors, each from 1,000 to 3,000 acres, managed by nobles and worked by commoners. The gap between these classes was wide. In a country with so much free land to the west, such a system could not prosper and eventually competition took its toll on privilege as the estates broke up. Out of the inadequacies of a feudal system on the frontier, there developed in Maryland not only broad social equality but a local self-government that made a great contribution to political self-sufficiency in America. The colonists here, as in New England, gained experience that served them well later on.

As Maryland became firmly established, there were multiplying pressures in England that were to result in further migration. By 1640, the breach between Parliament and Charles I had become too great to heal. The legislators assembled and refused to be dispersed for nine years, becoming known as the Long Parliament. By 1642, actual warfare broke out and the Puritan Revolution was in full swing. After resisting for four years the king surrendered and, in 1649, was executed. Oliver Cromwell now dominated the scene until he died. In 1660, Charles II was invited to the throne; the English were willing to try a monarch again. With his accession, colonial growth, which had been slowed in

previous years, speeded up. During the next quarter century, three more of the 13 colonies were established— Pennsylvania and the two Carolinas— and New Netherland, taken from the Dutch, became the English colonies of New Jersey and New York.

The Carolinas—strange sisters

In the spring of 1663, Charles II indicated that a new era in colonization was under way when he granted eight of his courtiers a generous slice of the Atlantic seaboard called Carolina. It was the greatest single unoccupied piece of land between Virginia and Spanish Florida, lying between the 36th and the 31st parallels. While the promoters put profit first, the move meant more than economic gain; it was a bold thrust at Spain. When in 1665 the charter was expanded to the 29th parallel, boldly taking in Spanish St. Augustine, Charles II indicated that England was again on the march in America. In this great real estate venture the proprietors planned to sell off portions of land.

Socially and politically, the founders hoped to reproduce English society in America with a structure comprised of nobles at the top and tenants and other dependents below. For a type of government favorable to their notions, they engaged the famous John Locke to prepare the Fundamental Constitutions of Carolina. It projected a strictly aristocratic way of life in a sparsely settled wilderness— a caste system with bluebloods in

In March, 1634, Maryland was settled by a group of 200 that included two Jesuits and many Roman Catholics from England. Painted by Emanuel Leutze.

complete control. For 20 years the proprietors forced their grand political document against the abrasive of frontier conditions, until it became a useless piece of parchment. Commoners who left England partially to avoid such conditions would have none of it. Southern Carolina was the scene of the more serious colonizing effort. In 1670, after several unsuccessful attempts farther north, a settlement called Charles Town was established. It would be relocated in 1680, on the present site of Charleston. The northern part of Carolina was not developed; it just grew. Its people were mainly small farmers of the independent frontier type, and they looked with suspicion upon the more feudal society south of them. It is not surprising that in 1691 Carolina was divided. The decision was a wise one, for as the 17th century progressed, South Carolina developed into a plantation, rice-raising type of colony, politically conservative and socially stratified. Its sister colony meanwhile expanded along quite different lines. Comprised largely of poor men, who strongly objected to any taxation, North Carolina was a land of smuggling, general lawbreaking, and extreme individualism. Both sections, however, had one important thing in common: They were peopled more by overflow from other American colonies than emigration from England, and provide an excellent example of that method of expansion in colonial America.

Other bits of patronage

When Charles II came to the throne after 12 years in exile and much in debt, he not only repaid loyal followers who had spent their own fortunes in his behalf by giving them huge grants of land in America. He also gave his brother, the Duke of York, the rich colony of New Netherland, recently wrested from the Dutch, stretching between the Connecticut and Delaware Rivers. It included a bit of real estate of great potential value known as Long Island. As in the case of the other proprietary colonies, the duke was to be the sole ruler, merely acknowledging feudal loyalty to the monarch by the annual payment of 40 beaver skins. There was no legislative body, and the only restraint upon York was the requirement that his laws conform fairly well with those at home. Obviously, he had a good deal of leeway.

From the beginning, New York, renamed by its new proprietor, was ruled by an iron hand. The duke, who was later to rule England itself as the unpopular James II, had ample opportunity to school himself in the fine points of being a king. The colony was recaptured by the Dutch in 1673, only to be returned one year later

This map titled A Description of the Towne of Mannados *shows Dutch New Amsterdam in 1661. As the English-owned colony of New York, it was governed by Sir Edmund Andros (above), 1674–81.*

as England triumphed over Holland. In the following years arbitrary government was resumed under the strict guidance of Sir Edmund Andros. In 1683, after years of complaint from the people, representative government came into being with the calling of the assembly. But due to disturbing delays, New Yorkers would have to wait almost another decade before they had any voice in their own affairs. Yet, despite the restrictiveness of its government, the colony developed well economically. Agriculture and trade increased, and an active commerce in furs with the Indians laid down a prosperous foundation.

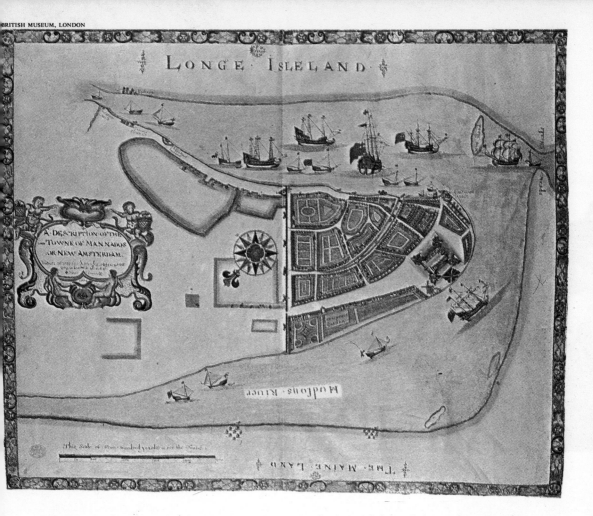

New Jersey resulted from the establishment of New York. Not long after the Duke of York received his charter, he signed over the land lying between the Hudson and Delaware Rivers to Lord John Berkeley and Sir George Carteret, who had helped greatly in restoring the Stuarts to the throne. The new proprietors, who were members of the original group that founded Carolina, named their new possession New Jersey in honor of one of them who had served as governor of the Island of Jersey. They were interested in their latest real estate venture primarily for profit. After a welter of sales and a resulting confusion of title claims, the proprietors finally surrendered their political powers to the crown in 1702. In the meantime, a curious assortment of Quakers, Catholics, and Presbyterians were in control of the little patch of land.

The Quakers buy in

Among the Quakers interested in New Jersey was a young man named William Penn. He had contributed to its new constitution of 1677, called the most liberal of its time, and had otherwise participated in the colonial experiment. When Penn's father died, Charles II owed him some 16,000

After William Penn's arrival in America in 1682, he established friendly relations with the Indians, as Benjamin West portrayed in this 1771 painting.

pounds, and in keeping with his policy of paying off in land, he now offered young William a sizable tract in America. Already interested in colonizing, Penn accepted and received his grant in 1681. The land, to which would soon be added three counties of Delaware (later partially separated from Pennsylvania in 1704), comprised an area almost as large as England itself. For this Penn owed the king nothing more than the customary beaver skins annually and one-fifth of any gold and silver he might discover. Nevertheless, he was more responsible to the king than either the Duke of York or Lord Baltimore.

A small council—elected by taxpayers from leading landowners—initiated bills, and a large elected assembly passed on them. But the governor had wide powers of appointment. The colony was in many respects a feudal domain, yet its proprietor was popular. One reason was the liberal government set up by the constitution. It provided for its own amendments, as does our own. Impeachment of officials offered a check on arbitrary power. Penn even suggested that laws inconsistent with the constitution were void, although it would be over 100 years before the courts would rule on unconstitutionality. Thus many motions advanced by the Quakers are a part of our law and tradition today.

The colonists who came to Pennsylvania suffered fewer physical hardships than earlier arrivals. Penn himself arrived in the fall of 1682, and within a year about 3,000 immigrants had landed and Philadelphia had 80 houses. Compared to other colonies, the Quaker settlement developed rapidly. There was plenty of food, little sickness, and no danger from the Indians. In 1684, the founder was obliged to return to England to settle a land dispute with Lord Baltimore. He did not return to America until 1699.

The same year Penn made his settlement, French explorers covered thousands of tortuous miles to lay claim to the Mississippi Valley. That spring Robert Cavelier de La Salle planted his nation's standard at the river's mouth and, calling the land Louisiana, claimed the American West. These events, in a single year, point up the differences in colonizing methods. As the two claims edged toward each other, empires would collide.

Georgia—buffer against Spain

By the end of the 17th century, the English had firmly established an unbroken line of colonies from New England southward to the Carolinas. As the proprietors of the latter had not heavily sprinkled their lands with settlers, and because Spain edged northward from Florida rather un-

certainly, the English decided to wedge in another colony. In 1732, George II granted a charter to a group of trustees headed by James Oglethorpe providing for a settlement to be named Georgia.

Political and religious developments in England dictated a change in methods of colonizing, and Oglethorpe's charter therefore differed from all others. In 1688, the English middle classes triumphed in the revolution of that year and promptly forced the passage of a toleration act granting freedom of public worship to dissenters. This meant that political and religious motives for colonization, once quite strong, were now minimized. Experience dictated still another modification: Time had shown that corporate colonies did not make a substantial profit for their sponsors. Also to the detriment of the mother country was the practice of granting wide political powers to these incorporators as a means of making their projects attractive to emigrants. All that resulted was a weakening of the hold upon such colonies.

Neither individual money-making, religious freedom, nor political independence were the prime movers; the forces at work behind this venture lay with the government itself. Oglethorpe was primarily a humanitarian, and his desire to empty the English jails of debtors coincided with the government's wish to plant a buffer colony snug against Spanish Florida. The charter provided that the trustees

*James Oglethorpe's humanitarian
idea brought men from the debtors' prisons to lands in Georgia.*

should get no personal gain from the
venture and must be under the strict
control of the crown, and that Georgia
would become a royal province within
21 years. Money for the project came
from two sources—funds solicited
from private philanthropic organizations and grants directly from Parliament. So the government of Georgia
was unlike its predecessors; it was
paternalistic in nature and controlled
from above. As in the case of the
others, however, frontier pressure finally led in 1751 to the granting of
assembly privileges. It was no real

step toward democracy, for a council
and governor, both appointed, held
the reins of power and the colony was
run by remote control.

How England kept her hold

From Jamestown to Georgia, for
125 years, the English carved out
colony after colony along the Atlantic
seaboard. These were years of experi-
mentation, of radically changing conditions at home, and of shifting international power. The result was three
principal types of ventures—royal,
proprietary, and chartered. With a
variety of people settling for diverse
reasons, it might seem that the result
would be a hodgepodge. But regard-
less of the patchwork appearance,
there were strong threads running
through the organizations, with the
ends securely held at home.

Whatever its type, each colony had
a governor, and while he was chief
executive of his own domain, he was
always the agent of the crown. Even in
the two charter colonies, where the
governor was elected, he was answer-
able to higher authority. In the proprietary colonies, where he received
his appointment from the proprietor,
his selection was first passed upon in
England. This official stood between
local legislatures, often liberal in attitude, and the mother country, whose
interests were at stake. Not only did
he represent the king directly in political matters; he was commander-in-
chief of the local militia and acted in
a diplomatic capacity by carrying on

*Oglethorpe's promise of a new beginning in a new world filled Europe's down-
trodden with hope. Among those who responded were persecuted Lutherans
from Salzburg, shown in this 1732 engraving as they depart for Georgia.*

relations with neighboring colonies. Furthermore, he could appoint vice-admiralty court judges, ordinary judges, justices of the peace, and sheriffs. All in all, his influence and powers were widespread and effective. Naturally, he was often the subject of bitter criticism from the independent-minded colonials who came to expect a no to their every request. Criticized in America, and often reprimanded by the home government, the governor's job was a lonely one. Inevitably perhaps, Americans later created a similar position for their own "colonies," and the same complaints echoed again from the Western territories in the 19th century.

Colonial connection with England was further extended in local legislatures. As a rule, it was the governor who called these bodies into session, although in some cases the legislature had the right to meet at least every three years despite the executive's wishes. However, no legislature could make a law effective without the governor's signature; in effect, he held an absolute veto. Should he not be inclined to exercise so direct a power, he could simply suspend a proposed law while he asked advice from the home government. The upper legislative house, called the council, was usually appointed, and almost without exception its members came from the more influential colonists of the upper classes. They were conservative in their thinking and more likely to have the monarch's interests at heart. The lower house, known as the assembly, was elected by colonial property owners and was therefore often similarly conservative. For example, in Pennsylvania one had to own 50 acres to be a qualified voter. While the lower house held the purse strings, as it does in our national government, and could wield great power, both the upper house and the governor had adequate means of checking any radical tendencies. One nuisance value the assembly often had was the right to earmark funds, which controlled the governor in his spending. Exercising the right did little to improve his disposition.

Despite the fact that the typical colonist wasn't treated as a first-class citizen, he managed—like the middle class in England—to nibble away at precedent and gradually gain more privileges. In the assembly his friends chipped away at the governor's position, worrying him about appropriating his pay, insisting that they alone had the authority to appoint the colonial treasurer, demanding the right to authorize military expeditions, and finally claiming they could send agents to represent them in London. While the assemblies did not always get their way, the seesaw battle edged in their direction. They were moving, slowly but certainly, toward a parliamentary form of government, and from their tribulations came experience that later served them well when the final break came with England. Gradually the friction of shifting conditions wore away at the string that held the colonial pearls together.

Spare the rod . . .

During the busy years of the 18th century, Mother England was like the old woman who lived in a shoe. She had so many children she didn't know what to do. But instead of spanking them soundly and putting them to bed, she fumbled and temporized. Members of the rapidly growing Empire family assumed that the customary "rights of Englishmen" were unaltered by distance from home. For decades, governing officials at London failed to challenge the assumption.

By the time they awakened to the fact that American colonists had accustomed themselves to a course of independent action in their day-to-day dealings, matters had gone too far to be corrected even by force. Men in America, long in the habit of shifting for themselves despite the attempts of colonial governors to check them, would not listen to disciplinary talk from faraway London. They had tasted the fruits of parental neglect, and they found the sensation to their liking.

THE FRENCH
AND INDIAN WARS

It was inevitable that England and France should clash in the New World. They had been in conflict for generations in Europe, and they had not improved their relations in North America, where their empires lay side by side. The struggle lasted for 70 years. It began in 1690 with the massacre by French and Indian raiders of English settlers at Schenectady, New York, and ended with the capture by the English of Quebec in 1759 and Montreal in 1760. Four colonial wars were fought within the 70-year span—King William's War, Queen Anne's War, King George's War, and the French and Indian War. This last and most important conflict gave its name to the whole series of wars. It began in 1754, and proved to be the beginning of the end of French power in North America. For despite their close alliances with the Indians, the French were never able to overcome the disadvantage of their small population in Canada and their lack of organized colonies. The English colonials were established settlers—family men willing to die defending their homes and farms.

THE REDCOATS

The English soldier at the left is a member of the 44th Foot, one of the regiments sent to America in 1755 to break French control of the Ohio Valley. They were commanded by General Braddock.

Sir Joshua Reynolds' young officer (right) is Captain Robert Orme, Braddock's favorite aide on the march into the Ohio country. He knew no more about wilderness warfare than his general did.

Braddock's men march through the wilderness in orderly European columns, to the sound of fife and drums. Their target is Fort Duquesne, the French base located on the site of present-day Pittsburgh.

The English expedition is ambushed by the French and Indians as they approach Fort

Duquesne. General Braddock would still not let his troops take cover in the Indian style.

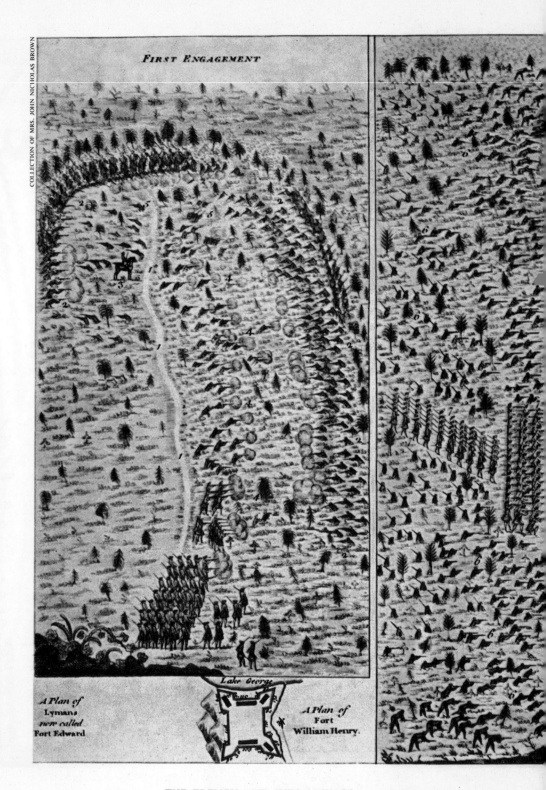

A Plan of
Lymans
now called
Fort Edward

A Plan of
Fort
William Henry.

THE FRENCH AND INDIAN WARS

THE BATTLE AT LAKE GEORGE

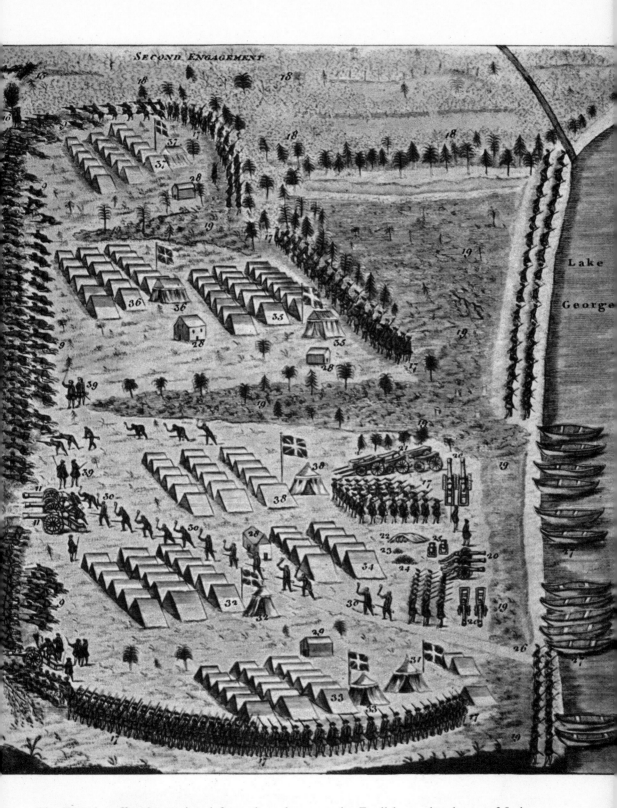

The French suffered a major defeat when they met the English on the shores of Lake George in 1755. In this print by an eyewitness, the English, in blue uniforms (left), were first surprised by a French ambush; later, in red uniforms (right), they triumphed.

115

LAKE CHAMPLAIN

LIBRARY OF CONGRESS

The French lost control of Lake Champlain in 1759, and in doing so, they opened to the English the southern route to Canada. English troops, led by Major General Jeffrey Amherst (opposite), took the important French forts controlling the lake—Crown Point (above) and Ticonderoga (below). Amherst was commander of the English forces in America. His portrait is by Reynolds.

NEW-YORK HISTORICAL SOCIETY

THE SIEGE OF QUEBEC

On the morning of September 13, 1759, the struggle for Quebec, capital of France's North American empire, began. The English army, commanded by Major General James Wolfe, had already engaged the French on the Plains of Abraham above the city, as British reinforcements were being brought ashore.

Louis Joseph, Marquis de Montcalm, led the French defense of Quebec. He was mortally wounded as the French began to lose their desperate battle to the English.

OVERLEAF: James Wolfe (center), surrounded by his officers as he lay dying on the Plains of Abraham, had lived long enough to see his English troops winning their battle with the French. Quebec, and with it all of French Canada, would soon fall. Wolfe is reported to have said, after he was shot, "Now God be praised. Since I have conquered, I will die in peace."

119

PUBLIC ARCHIVES OF CANADA

TRINITY CHURCH, SAINT JOHN, NEW BRUNSWICK

CHAPTER 5

STRUGGLE FOR POWER

The westward expansion of colonial America developed a sectional problem that was first to plague England and later influence the growth of the United States. As settlers moved inland from the coastal area and ascended the lower slopes of the Appalachians, they were separated from their neighbors to the east by waterfalls that prevented a navigable connection. If one were to draw a north-south line touching these falls, there would emerge what is called the fall line. As imaginary as the equator, it nevertheless divided the early settlers into the tidewater and piedmont residents. (The latter term refers to an up-country plateau lying between the fall line and the crest of the mountains.)

Piedmonters found that while communication with the coastal people was now more difficult, a north-south movement was relatively easy, and the continual flow of population up and down molded a section that could call itself Western. Corralled by geography, the newcomers banded together

The French coat of arms (top) once appeared on the gates of Quebec, and the British arms (bottom) hung in the city of Boston.

in common cause, and conscious of their remoteness and newness, hooted in derision at those who had been lucky enough to pre-empt seaboard sites. Often without regard to fact, they looked upon the tidewater people as "aristocrats" who were bent upon monopolizing power and privilege for themselves. It was the usual case of the majority clinging to what it had gained and the minority striving for what it wanted.

There was just enough truth in the frontiersmen's charges to make their cause sound plausible, particularly in the West. Many a small Western landowner was in debt to tidewater speculators for land he had bought. In addition to being hounded for payment, he was obliged to sell what few products he raised for profit to the speculators at whatever price was offered. The usual animosity of a debtor class to a creditor class resulted, and it is not surprising that those along the frontier convinced themselves that the economic game was rigged in favor of the dealers.

It was in this first West that an American population was born. While it was comprised of a number of na-

tionalities, English, German, and Scotch-Irish contributed the predominant strains. They were generally small farmers in a land almost wholly agricultural. There were no domains with their semi-feudal lords of the very early colonial type. The piedmonters lived in an isolation that not only demanded self-preservation but demanded it so strongly that ethnic lines were obliterated in the face of common defense. Outside forces like the elements and the Indians pressed this frontier into a compact ideological community.

Other straws that bound the clay of Western society were the dissatisfactions of its members with the Europe they had left. If they were not joined in a common dislike of the old country, they at least shared a lack of interest in it. The sentiment was not only to affect the course of English colonial development but to have deep influences on the later history of American diplomacy.

Western expansion had a long-range effect upon American development, and during the 18th and 19th centuries it showed up clearly on the national scene. Westerners on succeeding frontiers continued to be an independent, vocal lot, negotiating often with other foreign powers (especially Spain) in order to wring advantages first from England and later from the United States. They experimented freely in government, social organization, and even communal living, to the unfailing distaste of the more conservative East. By the end of the 19th century, American historians were talking about the significance of the West upon national growth, and universities were experimenting with courses dealing with the westward movement.

English pressure mounts

Until the middle of the 18th century, England made no effort to control the expansion of her American colonies. The more people of any nationality who buttressed her holdings, the stronger her relative position became. Spain had got off to a fast start in colonizing and had laid claim to

124

On April 9, 1682, La Salle reached the mouth of the Mississippi. Here he claimed the river and the lands it drained for Louis XIV of France, naming the huge territory Louisiana in the king's honor.

most of the Western Hemisphere. By 1700, the day of the conquistadors was about over and the first flush of conquest had abated. Most of the quick money had been milked from Spanish America, and in the days ahead a more solid economic basis would have to be found to make Spain's claims hold up. For over 200 years, since the days of Columbus, she had squandered her American gold, quarreling with other Continental powers.

The 18th century was to see the Spanish on the defensive and the English ever ready to contribute to their downfall. No fewer than eight times in a little over 100 years the two nations went to war. As Spain poured out her treasure, trying to keep back the intruders, England merely grew in stature and attained for herself the reputation of being

mistress of the seas. In 1763, in the Treaty of Paris, England got East and West Florida. By 1790, Spain was in such a weakened condition that her day as a great colonizer was nearly over.

As English colonists filtered through the Appalachian passes, pressing their claims against Spain's, another nation worried about such steady expansion. The Canadian French had swept around the northern end of England's colonial frontier and plunged deep into the continent along the Great Lakes and down the Mississippi Valley. Their American empire depended upon furs and thus was loosely organized with vast stretches of land between settlements. With the exception of the Iroquois, with whom they fought constantly, the French were friendly with the Indians. The natives generally could be counted upon as their allies.

This was important, for, like the Spanish, the French had been unable to populate heavily the lands they claimed. They realized their weakness as England's strong young offspring relentlessly pressed forward. To be prepared for the inevitable collision, the French tried a policy of containment by building a ring of forts around the oncoming English. From Fort Niagara in the north to Fort Toulouse on the Alabama River, they blocked out a line of defense. Crown Point, on Lake Champlain, was fortified to check any English overflow out of the valleys of the Connecticut or Hudson Rivers. But despite all precautions, the hold of the French was too weak to withstand much pressure. The English frontiersmen were on the prowl, backed by a colonial population much greater than that of their rivals.

King William lights the fuse

Nervously the French watched England's American colonies edge forward. Before the end of the 17th century they decided to check such growth before it became unmanageable. These were days of considerable uproar in England, and when in 1688 the Glorious Revolution fixed attention upon difficulties at home, the French made ready to strike. It was an opportunity not only to hurt the English colonies but also to humiliate the friends of the powerful Iroquois Indians. The ensuing conflict was known as King William's War. While it pitted England and France against each other in America, it was primarily European, for it was the accession of the Dutchman, William of Orange, to the English throne that touched off hostilities. His people already were fighting the French, and it was primarily his wish to involve England in the conflict that moved him to accept the throne.

Frenchmen in America welcomed the clash between the two European powers as an opportunity to conquer the English colonies, and in the winter of 1689–90, Count Louis de Frontenac, the governor of New France, lashed out at New York and New England. First his troops struck Schenectady, then the country between Maine and

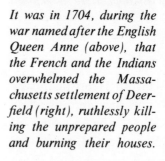

It was in 1704, during the war named after the English Queen Anne (above), that the French and the Indians overwhelmed the Massachusetts settlement of Deerfield (right), ruthlessly killing the unprepared people and burning their houses.

New Hampshire, and finally, Fort Loyal (the present Portland, Maine). Although New York was torn by rebellion against its own governor, common adversity drove the people in the Northern colonies together in defense. By May, 1690, a counterattack was launched that yielded up Port Royal in Acadia (now Nova Scotia) as a prize. During that summer Quebec itself was threatened but did not fall, and the war settled down to sporadic raids back and forth across the border. The Peace of Ryswick in 1697 required that each side return what it had captured; neither participant gained anything and no important questions were settled. An uncertain

peace ensued in Europe, but in America the French and English continued to spar. Shortly the gong would sound and round two would be under way.

War in the name of the queen

Within four years the European powers were fighting again. In 1700 the king of Spain died and was unforeseeing enough not to leave a direct heir. Sharp-eyed monarchs in other countries saw opportunity in this oversight and at once fell to battling over the successor, each hopeful of gaining an advantage. Louis XIV of France claimed the throne for his grandson and was at once opposed by England, Holland, Austria, and some of the German electorates that supported Leopold I, head of the Austrian house of Hapsburg. The conflict was properly labeled the War of the Spanish Succession, but in America the English honored their new sovereign by calling it Queen Anne's War. As most of Europe, as well as America, Asia, and Africa, was affected, the struggle was truly a world war. To most of the European nations who opposed France, it was a war to check the ambitions of Louis XIV, but to Holland and England it was a fight for colonies and commerce. During the years 1701 to 1713 the English concentrated their efforts on the American front in attempts to extinguish French claims on this side of the Atlantic.

American colonists received the news of more conflict with mixed feelings. Traders at Albany resented the development, for they had established a thriving business with Montreal, supplying the French with cheap trinkets for the Indians. So strong was their influence that a period of neutrality between New York and Canada existed during the early war years. Meanwhile the New England colonies, jealous over fishing rights off the Canadian banks and dissatisfied by their lack of gain in the previous war, enjoyed no peace. The French took advantage of friendship with the Indians and sent them against New England settlements without letup. The massacre at Deerfield, Massachusetts, in 1704, characterized the savagery of the coming struggle. Fifty-three killed and 111 prisoners was the high price the English paid in this raid. As the attacks increased, New Englanders asked the home government to conquer Canada as the only sure means of stopping the carnage. Accordingly, an expedition sailed against Port Royal in Acadia but accomplished nothing more than taking a few prisoners. In the following years attempts to storm the strongholds of New France were made both by land and sea with the same unsatisfactory results. Port Royal fell in 1710, as the British force outnumbering the French eight to one gained a rather empty victory. The next year another try was made, and a fleet carrying 12,000 men sailed to attack Quebec. Lost in a fog on the St. Lawrence River, the ships ran aground; 10 vessels and 900 men were the cost and not a blow was struck. Meanwhile the Spanish, now allied with the French, launched an attack from Florida and pressed the colony of South Carolina. The struggle in that sector saw the opponents so evenly matched that neither side won any decisive victories.

Peace breaks out again

In 1713, the Treaty of Utrecht ended the long struggle. France surrendered New Foundland and Acadia (except for Cape Breton Island) and all territory loosely described as Hudson Bay. France also recognized that the British were overlords of the powerful Iroquois. In a few years, however, the future looked a little less gloomy, and once more the French were hard at work empire-building. While the Treaty of Utrecht apparently gave a good deal to England, its terms were vague and territorial boundaries ill-defined. That knowledge was enough for her rivals; they dug furiously at the weak spots.

That the French were permanently undismayed by their American losses was made evident when they established the powerful Fort Louisbourg on Cape Breton. Located on an all-weather harbor, it stood poised to protect the residents of New France from naval invasion and to control

This flag, carried by New Englanders at Louisbourg in 1745, shows the symbol of England's military and naval power, Britannia, with spear and shield.

the northern fishing waters against all interlopers. So successful were the French in reviving their fishing industry that the Cape Breton region now prospered while New Foundland, recently lost to the English, declined.

The French wooed the Indians, sent their fur trappers plunging yet deeper into the American interior, and strove desperately to outsell English traders. Old posts in the Mississippi Valley, long in decay, were reactivated. If the English could not always see what was going on, they could feel it. Traders at places like Albany noticed that furs brought in by the Indians had declined sharply in quality; obviously the French were getting the best ones. The only answer to this was for the English to move farther west, into direct competition. It meant increased contact with the enemy, more friction, and renewed fighting. Despite that prospect, English traders surged forward and, encouraged by the Board of Trade at home, matched every move

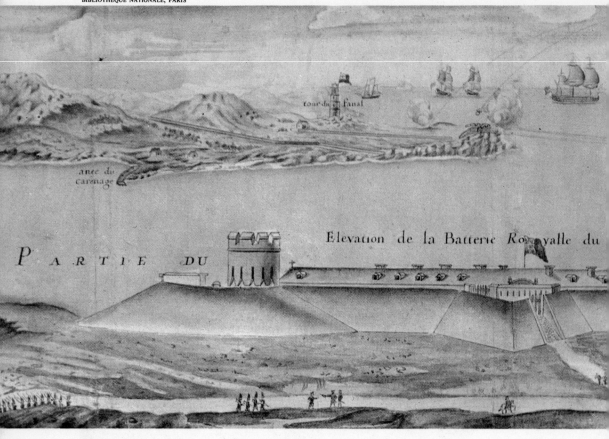

the French made. While trappers lived with the tribes, taking Indian wives and integrating with the natives to a degree not reached before, the Anglican church did its best to match the Jesuits by sending missionaries to work among the red men. When the mother countries would notify their colonial children that war was officially declared, the offspring would fly at each other with renewed vigor.

Captain Jenkins loses an ear

The Peace of Utrecht, like many other settlements, was only an armistice. Within 25 years Britain was again embroiled in war, and of course her American colonies took part. The trouble arose out of England's commercial aggressiveness, this time in South America. While attempting to break into Spain's trading monopoly, an English seaman, Captain Robert Jenkins, asserted that one of his ears had been cut off by Spanish officials. Exhibiting in England what he said was the severed ear, Jenkins caused a wave of resentment against such a national insult. By the spring of 1739, an undisguisedly imperialistic war against Spain was on. After four years of inconclusive fighting, France sided with Spain. Meanwhile, over in the second ring of

Batterie de l'Isle solennèe   *Isle Verte*   *Pointe a Rochefort*

terre   P O R T

The Royal Battery (foreground) was captured by the British from the French early in the 1745 battle at Louisbourg, but the Island Battery (center, right) held out until the end. Its guns are shown dueling with those of the Americans (background).

the European circus, another war was raging as the king of Prussia tried to wrest territory from the Austrian Queen Maria Theresa. By 1744, the wars had merged into a single grand conflict. Spain, France, and Prussia were now pitted against Russia, Holland, England, and Austria. Known in Europe as the War of the Austrian Succession, its American counterpart was named in honor of England's King George.

To the American colonies, the main feature of the war was England's conquest of magnificent Fort Louisbourg. The action took place in the spring of 1745 when a fleet of 90 vessels out of Boston besieged the fortification. After 49 days, during which 9,000 cannonballs were hurled into it, the stronghold surrendered. Furious, the French dispatched a large fleet to recover their lost prize and, in retribution, to burn Boston. Bad weather combined with bad management led to a dismal failure. When still another attempt was made, the British sent the French squadrons fleeing for home.

Clearly, naval warfare was not going to save France her colonies.

A temporary peace resulted from the Treaty of Aix-la-Chapelle in 1748, by which England traded the newly captured Louisbourg for the port of Madras, India, recently taken by the French. American colonists complained loudly when their prize was handed over to ransom a place on the other side of the globe. Massachusetts had voted 50,000 pounds for the expedition against Louisbourg. Supplies and men had come from other New England colonies also. The home government's attempt to mollify them with money was a failure. Already Americans were having difficulty taking the international point of view.

In peace, prepare for war

With the return of peacetime conditions, the English became increasingly active in America. Men of the Hudson's Bay Company moved far out on the Northwestern plains, building posts and trading in an area the French regarded as their preserve. Louisbourg, now back in French hands, was flanked by a new and powerful English fort at Halifax to match military strength. Over in the Ohio Valley the contest reached new proportions. While the English constantly strengthened their position, the French answered by building a series of forts around Lake Erie and on the Allegheny River. Governor Robert Dinwiddie of Virginia sent young George Washington in 1753 to order out the in-

terlopers, but they politely ignored him. The angry governor next dispatched Captain William Trent to build a post where the Allegheny and Monongahela Rivers joined to form the Ohio, and he was *not* ignored; the French threw him out and built Fort Duquesne. Once more Washington marched westward; this time he defeated the French and built Fort Necessity. But in 1754 the enemy captured it. With the outposts of the two nations in constant friction, enough heat was being generated to start another conflagration.

That the English were not yet ready for war was indicated by their offer to accept the Allegheny Mountains as their western boundary. All they wanted was part of Nova Scotia in return. Strangely, the French refused, and with the failure of diplomacy, the return to arms was inevitable. Despite peaceful efforts, both sides had long expected another war, and during the summer of 1754, active preparations were made. Meanwhile, representatives of seven English colonies, along with those of the Iroquois, met at Albany to work out plans for their mutual defense when hostilities were renewed. It was no spontaneous meeting. The English government sponsored it, at the request of the Board of Trade, with the hope of organizing all Indians south of the Great Lakes. The Iroquois were unhappy because they were not supported enough in their forays against the French. And what was worse, while the Indians were helping the English, the Virginians were stealing their lands.

The conference produced a plan for intercolonial organization, drawn up by Benjamin Franklin, known as the Albany Plan of Union. It proposed a "super colony," loyal to England but organized to simplify colonial administration and lend unity of effort. The proposal was unanimously adopted by the Albany Congress and unanimously rejected by the colonies involved. Despite such sharp disapproval, the notion of the Albany Plan was significant, for it recognized the need for American union, a thought that was to return to colonial minds within the next few years.

While the delegates debated at Albany, news of Fort Necessity's loss was received. The English wasted no more time in discussion; they sent General Edward Braddock to America with two regiments of redcoats. After a laborious journey through the wilderness, plagued by sickness and hard marching, Braddock's forces met the enemy in July, 1755, near Fort Duquesne. There the French and Indians, using the natural protection of trees and fighting guerrilla-style, slashed at the English forces until they were cut to pieces. With Braddock mortally wounded

General Edward Braddock, commander in the battle for Fort Duquesne in 1755, was shot through the lungs near the end of the struggle with the French and Indians and, as his army retreated, was carried for two days before he died.

This sketch of James Wolfe, made in 1759 at Quebec by an officer, George Townshend, is thought to be the best likeness of him.

and many of his troops dead or badly wounded, the long march home began. During that summer Governor William Shirley of Massachusetts led a similar expedition against Fort Niagara, only to be hurled back. The English now made ready in earnest. Seven thousand Acadians, now under their rule but considered a risk because of their French origin, were evacuated from their homes in Nova Scotia and scattered along the Eastern and Southern seaboard. Although their European parents were still at peace, the colonies in America were poised for an all-out struggle. In May of 1756, the starting signal was given in Europe and the Seven Years War was under way there. The American part of it was called the French and Indian War.

Seven fateful years

As usual, the European conflict arose out of jealousies and a struggle for power. Austria still had lingering grievances against Prussia from the previous war. As she plotted alliances against Prussia, that country turned to England for support. France promptly signed on with Austria, and the stage was set. In America, where preliminary sparring had gone on for two years, the principals were more than ready. The opening rounds of the main event were punishing ones for the English. In Europe, Frederick II of Prussia staggered under the combined blows of France, Russia, and Austria while the French won some sparkling engagements at sea. In the Western Hemisphere, French hopes rose as General Louis Joseph de Montcalm took command in Canada and chopped away at northern colonial outposts of England. These reverses, along with others in India, posed a serious problem for the British government and made it clear that some drastic reforms in military strategy must be carried out if there was to be any hope of victory in this international war.

The tide began to turn in 1757. William Pitt, the Great Commoner,

On July 26, 1758, English soldiers rowed into Louisbourg harbor and captured two French frigates guarding the fortress. One ship was taken (right), the other burned. For the second time, Louisbourg surrendered to the English.

took command of the British war effort and turned all his energies toward the pressing problems at hand. At home he engaged in a house cleaning that saw a number of older and less aggressive generals replaced by young and ambitious officers. Pulling out of the Continental theater as much as he could, Pitt focused his attention upon the American scene. By the following year young Major General Jeffrey Amherst and Brigadier General James Wolfe had recaptured the great Canadian fort of Louisbourg, opening the way to the St. Lawrence

Valley. Colonials in America were made more enthusiastic for the war by an increased recognition of their military men, a policy that considerably strengthened campaigning English forces.

By 1759, all was ready for a gigantic three-pronged assault upon the Canadian French. In this, "the wonderful year," the war was won as Wolfe moved against Quebec by way of the St. Lawrence River, and Amherst plunged toward the same objective by way of Lake Champlain, while a third contingent captured Fort Niagara. On the night of September 12, Wolfe put ashore 5,000 troops who, after scaling the heights before Quebec by night, stood ready for the final assault on the Plains of Abraham next morning. In a historic battle both Wolfe and Montcalm lost their lives, but victory went to the English. Five days later the city of Quebec surrendered. Only Montreal, the last French stronghold, remained; it fell during the next year. With that surrender, in the autumn of 1760, the British gained practical control of all Canada.

France wanted to make peace. But she had commitments to her European allies, who opposed treating on that subject with England. Maria Theresa of Austria wanted her hated enemy Frederick II of Prussia crushed, and as the French troops were carrying on a fairly successful, though expensive, campaign against the Prussians, she wanted to continue the war. France now turned to Spain and convinced Charles III, who had recently come to power, that England ought not to dominate the North American scene. By the Family Compact that followed, the Spanish entered the war against the English in 1761. Pitt now became thoroughly stubborn about peace talks and pushed the war effort until he forced his opponents to give up the struggle. France lost West Indian bases; Spain lost Havana and Manila. By the end of 1762, they were willing to listen to Pitt's proposals.

The rewards and costs of war

When the diplomats gathered at Paris in February, 1763, to make peace, significant changes were in the offing. At one stroke France gave up an empire when it signed over Canada to the English. Another huge slice of land was fully surrendered as she gave up any further claim to territory between the Alleghenies and the Mississippi River. Spain, once again helping the French Bourbons fight their wars, paid the price of involvement by surrendering Florida and any rights she had east of the Mississippi in order to regain Cuba. The French regained the sugar islands of Martinique, Guadeloupe, and St. Lucia, but as far as North America was concerned, they were forever finished.

Because of the territory she gained, both in America and elsewhere, Great Britain emerged as the most powerful nation in the world. Henceforth her westward movement across America was to be unhindered by any other European power. American colonists, eager to expand and to speculate in Western lands, looked upon this development with great anticipation. When they discovered that Mother England had other plans for the newly acquired territory, their happiness turned to sullen gloom. But men in England, intoxicated by their country's meteoric rise to wealth and power, did not hear the mutterings across the Atlantic.

METROPOLITAN MUSEUM OF ART

Bruton Parish Church, in 18th-century Williamsburg, painted by Woodworth Thompson.

LIFE IN
COLONIAL AMERICA

From the forests of Maine to the marshes of Georgia, the men and women who immigrated to America pursued the great lure of the New World—equality of opportunity. Some stayed along the coast, where the Atlantic, an abundant fishing ground and the passageway to the rich markets of Europe, brought them wealth. Here, working in the growing cities of Boston, New York, Philadelphia, and Charleston, tradesmen prospered and artisans found outlets for their talents. Others drifted inland, attracted by the soil that was theirs if their courage was great and their backs strong. From the wilderness they carved farms and homesteads that became the foundations of villages and towns. In the South, vast plantations based on slavery, an incongruous element of colonial life, grew and flourished. There were sharp differences in the ways of life, the philosophies, and the governments of the various colonies. But united by common problems and swept on by the tide of common successes, colonists of different nationalities were transformed into a new breed—Americans.

137

COLONIAL TYPES

Among the leading citizens of aristocratic Charleston was Ralph Izard, a wealthy Huguenot planter. The double portrait (above) of Izard and his wife was painted in 1775 by John Singleton Copley.

The adultlike Sunday-best clothing of Pilgrim and Puritan youngsters is seen in the painting of the sober-faced Mason children (left) done around 1670 by an unknown artist in Massachusetts.

The Quaker settlers were persecuted and harassed in New England and New York. But men and women like those painted by Nicolino Calyo (right) later found freedom of worship in early Pennsylvania.

Baltimore was just a village when the picture above was painted in 1752. By 1776, however, it was a busy seaport and the ninth-largest city in the colonies.

The center of Boston's commercial district was State Street (right). It was in front of the Old State House (center) that the Boston Massacre took place.

The South's most prosperous port was Charleston (below), where ships were loaded with profitable cargoes of indigo and rice from the inland plantations.

CENTERS OF COMMERCE

A NEW METROPOLIS

The most enterprising and attractive of the 18th-century American cities was bustling Philadelphia. The heart of it was the junction of Second and High Streets, marked by the spire of Christ Church. Distances to other cities were measured from this intersection, shown below in an engraving from a 1799 series by Thomas Birch.

THE BOUNTIFUL OCEAN

Along the New England coast, where fishing and trade provided jobs and income for thousands, a powerful and wealthy merchant class came into being. Cod fishing, which had brought European fishermen to New Foundland and New England waters in the past, was now a lucrative industry in the colonies. The drawing at the right, made around 1720, illustrates how the cod were caught, cleaned on large stages, salted, and dried for sale after the valuable oil had been removed from the livers of the fish. (See legend at the top.)

MUSEUM OF FINE ARTS, BOSTON

Merchant John Amory, above in a Copley portrait, made a fortune in Boston but left America when the Revolution began. The great success of the colonial mariners angered their British competitors, who insisted that Parliament tighten restrictions on New World commerce.

Yankee seamen, like the one at the right from *A Book of Trades, or Library of Useful Arts,* protested loudly when the English attempted to limit their activities. The result was downright evasion of the law, through smuggling or other means, and a stiffening of resistance to the crown.

NEW YORK PUBLIC LIBRARY

View of a Stage & also of y̆ manner of Fishing for, Curing & Drying Cod at NEW FOUND LAND.
The Habit of y̆ Fishermen. B. The Line. C. The manner of Fishing. D. The Dressers of y̆ Fish. E. The Trough into
ͪ they throw y̆ Cod when Dressed. F. Salt Boxes. G. The manner of Carrying y̆ Cod. H. The Cleansing y̆ Cod. I. A Press
ͬract y̆ Oyl from y̆ Cods Livers. R. Casks to receive y̆ Water & Blood that comes from y̆ Livers. L. Another Cask to receive
ͥ. M. The manner of Drying y̆ Cod.

A. DEVANEY

This "sacred cod" carving hangs in the Massachusetts State House.

Indians and British soldiers are among the guests depicted in the painting, *Colonial Wedding in Virginia* (above). Ladies and bewigged gentlemen wave farewell to the departing newly-weds, while the bride's mother sobs into her handkerchief and Indians watch impassively.

LIFE IN COLONIAL AMERICA

TOBACCO FOR ENGLAND

Virginia's prosperity was based on tobacco and was therefore dependent on
the slaves who worked in the fields. In
this old water color (left), the slaves
dance and relax during a work respite.

The 1784 drawing (right) pictures a
wharf where tobacco was loaded for shipment abroad. For years tobacco was better
than money in Virginia, and Church of
England ministers drew their salary in it.

THE GREAT PLANTATIONS

The half-century before the Revolution was the Golden Age of Virginia. Planters lived elegantly on their tidewater estates, which encompassed thousands of acres. The plantation shown here consisted of a great house, slave cabins, barns, warehouses, and a water mill.

CHAPTER 6

SEEDS OF REVOLUTION

When the sounds of cannonading in the Seven Years War died away, there was revealed along the Atlantic seaboard a new nationality. For more than a century an American strain had been developing, so imperceptibly that many in America as well as the Old World were unaware of it. Only when England tried to exercise increased control did the colonists realize that an individual society, ready to demand more freedom, had arisen. The war itself had not only awakened them to their potentialities, but its result had freed them from fear of the French and Spanish. Only the Indians stood between them and unlimited expansion. It is little wonder that they began to flex their biceps and assert themselves. In some respects, the American Revolution had started.

For some years England's tightening restrictions had annoyed the colonists. To strike out at her commercial rivals, England had introduced a series of laws known as

King George III, English ruler during the American Revolution, as he appeared in his coronation robes. Painted by Allan Ramsay.

the Navigation Acts. They conformed to the prevailing economic theory of Europe called mercantilism. Commercially active Continental countries acquired as much bullion as possible through trade, particularly with their own colonies, over which they had complete control. They strengthened themselves with this treasure and often used it to finance wars against their neighbors. It was with the same idea of making their empire self-sufficient that the British turned toward mercantilism.

The first act, passed in 1650, was designed primarily to curb the Dutch, who had captured a large portion of the carrying trade. All foreign vessels were forbidden to trade with the English colonies. Within a year the law was tightened to force goods from the colonies into English vessels only. Ten years later, in 1660, and again in 1663, additional provisions stated that not only were all foreign merchants excluded from the English colonies, but certain "enumerated" goods, like sugar, cotton, indigo, and tobacco, must be transported to England before they could be sold elsewhere. By a law of 1673, ships bound for England from the colonies, bearing any of the enumerated goods, were required to post a bond to insure delivery of the goods in an English port as promised. The law also required that duties be paid at the point of shipment. These acts were crowned by the statute of 1696, which tightened the existing laws to the extreme. Henceforth no colonial goods might be carried from one colony to another except in English-built ships. Governors were threatened with heavy fines for allowing infractions, and any colonial laws that conflicted with the act were declared null and void. The better to enforce its edict, the English government now separated the American colonies into two admiralty divisions and appointed judges to each to deal with violators. This final attempt must have been effective, for at once trade between the colonies and England soared.

The Navigation Acts, although aimed at the Dutch, were enacted also to assure English traders a monopoly in America. The Northern colonies were those most interested in trade, and they welcomed the acts of 1650–51, for the Dutch were their chief competitors. Under the law, vessels of New England were regarded as English, and as the mother country did not have enough ships to carry the products herself, colonial shipowners gladly supplied the remainder. New England quickly became an active trading center, and its merchants engaged in direct commerce with European nations, blandly ignoring the restrictive acts of 1660 and 1663, and shipping enumerated goods when and where they pleased. Only extreme internal dissension and warfare at home kept England from enforcing her commercial laws.

England's restrictive legislation, though often ignored by the colonists, served to drive the two societies apart. Laws demanding that an American merchant first bring his goods to England before selling them elsewhere could be evaded. But when the home government closed its markets to American agricultural products, there were no means of trading oats, wheat, beef, or bacon for English hardware or textiles. Although the colonials were forbidden to manufacture, this kind of legislation forced them to it. Short-sighted Englishmen could not see that with a plentiful supply of iron, wool, and wood, the Americans could easily turn to the production of manufactured articles. English restrictive legislation merely hastened the process and inadvertently pushed Americans toward self-sufficiency.

Imperial England's new discipline

At the Peace of Paris in 1763, England found that she had taken a gigantic leap forward as a world power and colonizer. Problems of administration and control over this

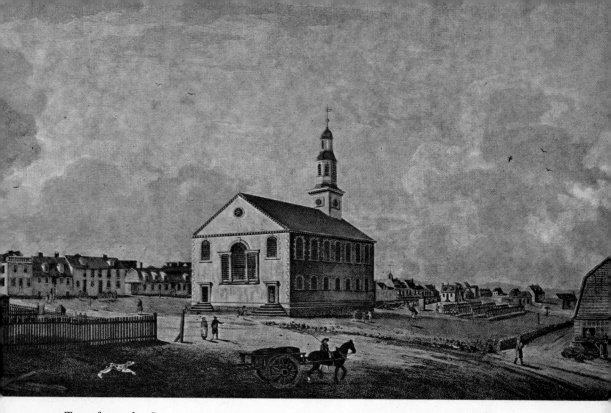

To enforce the Sugar Act, Parliament ruled that colonial merchants accused of smuggling were to be tried in the admiralty courts in Halifax, Nova Scotia.

global domain now put her in a serious mood; no longer would haphazard methods suffice to run the imperial firm. A glance at the exchequer revealed that the national debt had almost doubled since Braddock marched toward Fort Duquesne. Taxation in England had mounted steadily, and new sources of income were becoming scarce. Why not ask the colonials for financial help? Large amounts had been spent in their defense, and more would be needed to protect them in the future against the Indians. To this the colonists objected. In their opinion, they had already contributed rather heavily and were then in debt about 750,000 pounds. If wages and profits were counted, the colonies annually contributed 2,000,000 pounds to England in addition to taxes. To them, it seemed enough. The English government was not to be put off, however. Money was needed, and it must be forthcoming. Orders went out to stiffen the customs collections, make the much-disobeyed Molasses Act of 1733 effective, extend stamp duties to America, further restrain colonial manufacturing, add more enumerated goods to the list of exports from America, and forbid colonials to issue paper money. These ideas were not hatched suddenly. Government officials had deliberated upon future fiscal requirements. In 1763, the ministry asked the Board of Trade a series of questions about the more efficient operation of the

The Stamp Act of 1765 brought a violent reaction from Americans. In the woodcut above, a group of New Hampshire citizens hangs a stamp agent in effigy. At the left is an engraving from a 1794 German almanac that gives the strong reaction of a group of patriots in Boston who burned the stamps. At the right is the stamp that caused the trouble.

empire. These concerned the type of government best suited to colonies, the number of soldiers necessary for adequate protection, the amounts of money that ought to be expected from the colonies for such protection, and finally, how best could England gain profit from her new territorial acquisitions.

The general result of this study was the Proclamation of 1763. It recommended that the "civilized" part of the new territory be given governments similar to those of the earlier colonies. Accordingly, Canada, East Florida, and West Florida now came into the colonial sphere. "Uncivilized" portions, such as Indian country lying west of the Appalachians, were to be reserved for the aborigines; only licensed traders could deal with them. By the drawing of this imaginary line between the settled and unsettled parts of the colonies, many a hopeful American speculator was cut off from what he thought would be a lucrative investment in land. Over loud objections, the English nevertheless fixed the line, hoping to check the westward movement until the government thought expansion both safe and wise. Officials were soon to learn, as did those of the United States later on, that the Americans were not to be fenced in. No set of laws would ever be devised to check the surging frontiersmen; they broke them as a matter of course.

More laws to break

Other recommendations made to the ministry resulted in specific financial legislation designed to produce greater revenues. In 1764 the Sugar Act was passed. Although it lowered the duty rates set in 1733, under the Molasses Act, it provided extensive regulations concerning collection. Ship captains had to post bonds to insure delivery of their cargoes, and illicit trade was to be ferreted out and stopped. Americans had no objection to the *passage* of such legislation, but they were incensed to think that the government planned to *enforce* it. Smuggling had become a time-honored calling along the Atlantic seacoast, and now it was in jeopardy.

During recent wars colonials had issued paper money, which had decreased in value. Debtors in America attempted to pay off their obligations in England with this money, and thus actually avoid payment of the entire amount. The Currency Act of 1764 put a stop to the issuance of fiat money and presented Americans with the problems of paying Englishmen what they owed in coin of the realm. Angered, the colonials resolved to buy less in England and to use products made at home. The seriousness of this intent is seen in the vow of Yale College students to buy no more imported liquors; henceforth they would patronize home industry only.

The Stamp Act of 1765 is another example of the attempt to raise more money in the colonies. Revenue stamps had to be bought for legal documents issued in America, or for the sale of such items as dice, playing cards, newspapers, calendars, and almanacs. The act roused heated opposition, despite England's claim that the taxes would be put into a defense chest for the colonies. Many who sympathized with England's financial distress complained that a new and unfair principle was involved. It was one thing to tax imperial commerce, but quite another to levy against items wholly American.

Even before news of the Stamp Act reached America, another disturbing piece of legislation was foisted upon the colonials. Called the Quartering Act, it required civil authorities to provide barracks and supplies for British soldiers. The government felt that the number of troops to be sent across the Atlantic would far exceed the available military quarters. New Yorkers saw at once that they would be hard hit, for the British army's North American headquarters was in their colony. So disproportionate would be the load that the legislature refused to carry out certain provisions of the act. Word was sent to the governor from England that he was to sign no laws until the legislators yielded. After a stalemate lasting several months, the New Yorkers gave in. But they did not forget that they had been forced, and resentment against the British government ran high.

Mob action

As restrictive laws rained down upon them, the colonists reacted with rage and violence. Individuals spontaneously banded together, and mob action was the order of the day. During the summer of 1765, young men calling themselves Sons of Liberty roamed the streets of Boston jeering at British officials and looking for trouble. In August, a mob entered the office of the admiralty court's deputy registrar, burned his records, and proceeded to the wine cellar of another customs official. After sampling liberally of his royal wares, "being enflam'd with Rum & Wine . . . [they] proceeded with Shouts to the Dwelling House of the Hon-l. Thos. Hutchinson, Esq., Lieut. Governor, & enter'd in a voyalent manner." As the invaders broke down the lieutenant governor's front door with axes, the startled official jumped from his supper table and fled to the shouts of "Damn him, he's upstairs. We'll have him yet!" By morning the house was burned out, its walls partly caved in, and a section of the roof gone. The rioters had melted into the population, and the government's offer of a reward for their delivery was never claimed.

Perhaps it was more than patri-otism, heightened by libations in the wine cellar, that fired up the zealots. In nearby Rhode Island, young ladies had notified the world that they would refuse the attentions of any man who voiced approval of the Stamp Act. Such a powerful interdict was bound to have its influence. Those who were unconcerned over the embargo on affections found excitement in mass meetings, parading, and shouting general disapproval of authority. The feeling was infectious, and even conservative men decided that under such a serious threat to their liberties they were "not averse to a little rioting."

The rights of Englishmen

Widespread protest over England's restrictive legislation was not confined to house-wrecking and window-smashing. The General Court of Massachusetts officially protested, saying that the Sugar Act would ruin the New England fisheries. Molasses, from the Caribbean islands, was an important part of the triangular trade the merchants carried on, and the new tax promised to hurt that thriving commerce. To Bostonians like Samuel Adams, the Sugar Act was more than an English economic measure; it threatened colonial political liberties. If trade could be taxed, then why could not everything the colonials had be taxed? This meant an end to self-government, guaranteed by many a colonial charter.

Virginians felt the same appre-

After the repeal of the noxious Stamp Act in 1766, this English print shows government members as a mournful group carrying the dead act to its grave.

hensions. In May, 1765, legislators at Williamsburg registered a sharp objection known as the Virginia Resolves. Twenty-nine-year-old Patrick Henry presented the resolutions, and after listening to his impassioned oratory, in which cries of "Treason" were heard among the listeners, the House of Burgesses reluctantly approved. In general the resolutions were a recitation of the rights of Englishmen, from the time of the first American settlement, and an insistence that those rights had been transferred to these shores with the immigrants. Foremost in the heritage, the most inalienable among the rights, was the privilege of being taxed by one's own representatives. As for Virginia, Henry held that its legislators, locally elected, were the only ones with the right to tax their people.

Word of the action spread up and down the seacoast. The Virginia Resolves were thought by New Yorkers to be too treasonable for publication, but New Englanders had no such

157

George Grenville (left) as prime minister pushed through the Stamp Act; Charles Rockingham (center), his successor, repealed it; and Charles Townshend (right), a later chancellor of the exchequer, created new colonial taxes.

qualms. By June they appeared in a Newport paper and shortly thereafter in several Boston newspapers. Sir Francis Bernard, governor of Massachusetts, said that at first he thought the people would submit to the Stamp Act but that the publishing of the Virginia Resolves "proved an Alarumbell to the disaffected." John Adams went further. He said that to the author of the resolutions went credit for starting the American Revolution.

The Stamp Act Congress

The Resolves surprised New Englanders. Virginia, the Old Dominion, was regarded as the most loyal of His Majesty's colonies and the least likely to be disobedient. For the moment, the Southerners appeared to have taken the initiative, and not to be outdone in patriotism, the General Court of Massachusetts now asked for delegates from all colonies to meet at New York in October to consider resistance to the Stamp Act. There was only a weak response, and four of the colonies, including Virginia, did not even send anyone to the Stamp Act Congress. Its members agreed that Englishmen in America had the same rights as those in England and could not be taxed without their consent. They protested against the system of trying violators without juries in the admiralty courts. All Englishmen, they said, had the right of trial by their peers. The gathering of delegates, from South Carolina to Massachusetts, indicated that despite their mild approach there was a growing community of sentiment, and that out of the crucible of common grievance there would emerge a new people. For the first time, a genuinely representative convention of the American colonies had acted in unison.

England backs down

Early in 1766, Parliament repealed the Stamp Act. It was not because its members were cowed by violence from across the Atlantic or by insistence upon rights. Aside from the fact that officials experienced a nightmare of confusion and non-cooperation in trying to make collections, there were increasing complaints from English merchants that business was declining. Colonials had resolved not to import from the mother country until some of her legislation was rescinded, and the result was noticeable. Within 20 months exports to America fell off by half. George III was at the same time tiring of his prime minister, George Grenville, who constantly lectured him about his responsibilities and otherwise annoyed him. While the king floundered, Parliament moved toward repeal. One of its members, a merchant, got to the root of the matter when he wrote to Lord Charles Rockingham, who had succeeded Grenville, "Our trade is hurt; what the devil have you been doing? For our part, we don't pretend to understand your politics and American matters, but our trade is hurt; pray remedy it, and plague you if you won't." By March, 1766,

MAGNA *Britannia: her Colonies* REDUC'D

In 1767, Benjamin Franklin had this cartoon made and sent to his friends. It prophesies the plight of England with her American colonies cut off.

The BLOODY MASSACRE perpetrated in King——Street BOSTON on March 5th 1770 by a party of the 29th REG.

Engrav'd Printed & Sold by PAUL REVERE BOSTON

UnhappyBoston! see thy Sons deplore,
Thy hallow'd Walks besmear'd with guiltless Gore:
While faithless P—n and his savage Bands,
With murd'rous Rancour stretch their bloody Hands;
Like fierce Barbarians grinning o'er their Prey,
Approve the Carnage, and enjoy the Day.

If scalding drops from Rage from Anguish Wrung,
If speechless Sorrows lab'ring for a Tongue,
Or if a weeping World can ought appease
The plaintive Ghosts of Victims such as these;
The Patriot's copious Tears for each are shed,
A glorious Tribute which embalms the Dead.

But know Exte summons to that awful Goal,
Where JUSTICE strips the Murd'rer of his So,
Should venal C—ts the scandal of the Lar
Snatch the relentless Villain from her Han
Keen Execrations on this Plate inscrib
Shall reach a JUDGE who never can be bri

The unhappy Sufferers were Mess. Sam. GRAY SAM. MAVERICK, JAM. CALDWELL, CRISPUS ATTUCKS & PAT. C.
Killed. Six wounded; two of them (CHRIST. MONK & JOHN CLARK) Mortally

Paul Revere's engraving of the Boston Massacre of 1770 was colonial propaganda. It claimed seven men were killed; actually five Americans lost their lives. The five coffins, drawn by Revere, were used on broadsides about the dead patriots.

a remedy was found; the act was rescinded.

Townshend and his duties

To no one's great surprise, William Pitt succeeded Rockingham as prime minister, but to the astonishment of many, including the recipient, Charles Townshend received the appointment as chancellor of the exchequer. Those who had hoped he would have only minor influence in the government were further dismayed when shortly Pitt was incapacitated by illness and Townshend became the power behind the scenes. As a member of Parliament, he had voted for both the passage and the repeal of the Stamp Act; now he veered once more and announced he was in favor of the act after all. Early in 1767, at the consideration of the budget, he assented to a proposal that would tax the colonies heavily so that levies against English landholders might be reduced. Members of the House of Commons, many of whom were property owners, expressed pleasure when he described how additional revenues could be gained by tightening customs regulations in America and laying on additional duties. His Revenue Act of June laid a tonnage tax on all vessels entering colonial ports and applied duties to such manufactures as glass, painters' lead, and paper, as well as tea. During the same month another act ordered the reorganization of the American customs service and the creation of additional admiralty courts. This last piece of legislation particularly infuriated the Americans, who continued to insist upon trials by jury.

John Adams defended British soldiers tried for murder for their part in the Boston Massacre. Portrait, Charles Willson Peale.

Vox populi and violence

Townshend, who died before the Revenue Act became effective, probably would have been surprised to hear the abuse piled upon his head for his program. He might have been flattered to learn that the principal objection to it by the colonials was that it worked. Smuggling came almost to a halt and customs revenues soared. One of those affected was John Hancock, a well-known Boston shipper, who paid little attention and no money to the authorities who demanded duty payments on the wine he imported. When his sloop *Liberty* was seized for nonpayment of customs, officials were roughly handled by angry crowds, their houses stormed, and one of their small boats carried triumphantly to Boston Commons, where it was burned. Incidents such as this caused England to send more officials as well as additional troops.

Day after day the tension mounted. Finally, on the evening of March 5, 1770, the inevitable occurred. A false fire alarm had drawn many people out into the streets, and as the mob surged back and forth, one of its members hurled a snowball at one of the stiff-backed British sentries. After being hit several times, he called for aid and got it. The angry crowd now moved closer, clubs were swung, a soldier was knocked down, shots were fired, and then in the shocked silence that followed, Bostonians saw five of their own lying dead or dying.

On September 30, 1768, a British fleet, shown in the engraving below by Paul Revere, anchored in Boston harbor. The next day soldiers of the 14th and 19th Regiments debarked at the Long Wharf and marched up King Street.

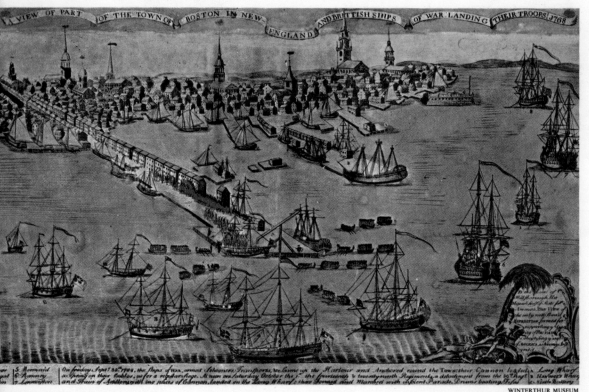

162

In 1774, Samuel Adams used some private government letters to incite rebellion. Benjamin Franklin was held responsible, and he was arraigned in England by the Privy Council (above) for allowing the letters to become public.

History would record it as a massacre. The affair might have attracted only short-lived attention had it not been for the artful way in which

Samuel Adams fanned the flames of fury at a town meeting. So great was the effect of his oratory that Governor Thomas Hutchinson acceded to

163

his demand that British troops be withdrawn from the city of Boston to islands in the harbor.

Although Lord North had addressed the House of Commons concerning partial repeal of the Townshend duties on the very day of the Boston Massacre, events had moved too far for such belated apologies to satisfy Americans. Months before blood was shed, it became clear to them that England proposed legislative interference as well as stricter economic control in the colonies. In 1768, the Massachusetts assembly circularized other colonies on the question of joint action against the home government for its invasion of their rights. Several legislatures passed acts of condemnation, some of which were based on the Virginia Resolves of 1769. Men like John Dickinson, who wrote a series of letters purportedly by a Pennsylvania farmer, contributed to a united sense of resentment. His writings were read in all parts of the colonies. In the weeks that followed the Boston Massacre, Samuel Adams provided some organization to the letter writers by setting up Committees of Correspondence. The plan was designed to provide nearby towns with information about the progress of events in Boston, but it soon was used as a model in neighboring colonies. Ultimately it would itself become an instrument of revolution, spreading news, assisting in intercolonial organization, and laying a

groundwork for new governments.

Angered colonials did more than write letters to each other about their rising discontent. They remembered that nonimportation of goods had resulted in the repeal of the Stamp Act, and they now applied the same pressure to the Townshend Acts. Merchants organized associations pledged not to import any goods that might be taxed by Parliament to raise revenue in America. Although members of Parliament insisted they were not responding to pressure, they shortly repealed the duties on

Abraham Whipple (left) was one of the Providence merchants who destroyed the British schooner Gaspee *(above) in 1772. During the Revolution, he was a privateer and once captured 10 British ships in 10 successive nights.*

lead, glass, and paper. To maintain the principle of taxing the colonies, however, they retained the tax on tea, feeling that this would harm no one. Americans were happy that their embargo had once again forced England to retreat, but the method was not without cost. Nonimportation meant a rise in the price of goods already in America, and the consumer often paid heavily for his patriotism.

The partial repeal of the Townshend Acts in 1770 proved to be a temporary sop. Merchants were happy over a restoration of normal business relationships, and conservatives were relieved that another crisis had passed. Restless souls like Sam Adams grew discouraged. No one seemed excited about the cause of personal liberty any more. But just when Adams feared that the spirit of resistance was dying, Lieutenant William Dudingston of His Majesty's customs schooner *Gaspee* came to the rescue.

Rhode Islanders, of independent mind from the start, greatly resented British interference with their smuggling. One June afternoon in 1772,

On December 16, 1773, 150 thinly disguised Boston patriots boarded English ships and dumped 342 chests of tea into the harbor. An 1846 print by N. Currier.

administration of the levy, and the theory behind it, irritated colonials. This violent action deeply angered Lord North and his associates, who regarded such conduct as a flouting of constituted authority.

Reaction from the government was prompt and drastic. In March, 1774, Lord North asked Parliament to take steps to fasten discipline more firmly on the colonies. The prime minister made it clear that the gauntlet had been thrown down by the Americans and severe punishment was called for. General Thomas Gage thought four regiments would suffice; Parliament answered with four coercive acts. The first closed the Port of Boston. The Massachusetts Government Act revoked the colony's charter and placed its administrative officers directly under royal control. An Administration of Justice Act provided that any British official charged with a capital offense in putting down a riot or collecting revenue should be sent to England for trial. (because of the known hostility of the colonial bench and bar). A fourth law revived the Quartering Act of 1765, but this time it said that *occupied* buildings might be used to house troops. Additionally, there was the Quebec Act, extending Canada's boundary to the Ohio River and taking over an area in which Virginia, Connecticut, and Massachusetts all had claims. When these laws had been put into effect, George III remarked, "The die is now cast; the colonies must either submit or triumph." For a monarch whose opinions were not always sound, this was prophetic.

The opposition unites

Colonial irritations had steadily mounted for some time. Scattered incidents had caused anger, but there was no compelling motive for all-out resistance. The coercive acts pulled the trigger. In September delegates from every colony except Georgia met at Philadelphia determined to offer united resistance. After they had adopted a declaration of rights, they got down to the more practical aspects of their business. They formed a Continental Association pledged to enforce nonimportation of any English goods. Although the delegates from Massachusetts were in a mood of violence—and probably agreed with Patrick Henry, who announced that "Government is dissolved . . . We are in a state of nature"—most of those present were not yet ready for

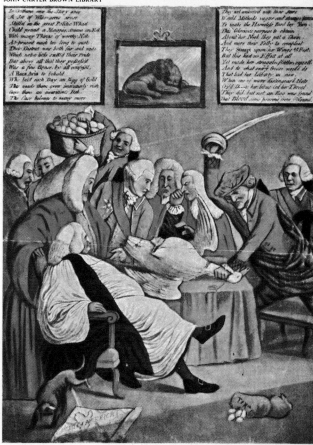

English ministers kill the goose—meant to be American—that lays the golden eggs.

revolution. At the moment they were principally interested in resistance to what they believed to be a violation of their rights as Englishmen and resolved to fight against coercion. When cooperation in this resolve was assured, they adjourned, and agreed that they would meet again the next May, if still coerced.

By that time shots had been fired and blood let, and whether the colonists liked it or not, the Revolution was under way.

MAIN TEXT CONTINUES IN VOLUME 3

The Pilgrim and Puritan Fathers

A SPECIAL CONTRIBUTION BY
A. L. ROWSE

The early founders of America, men of strong faith and convictions, came from England and built a tradition of simplicity and hard work that helped to shape the direction of the nation.

The New England Puritans had already behind them almost a century's experience of Protestant effort and thought. What was new, and of extreme importance, was the opportunity to carry these ideas into practice. This ideal was the dynamic motive that drove the Puritans across the Atlantic.

Even in New England, the Puritans were a small minority, when one considers effective church membership. But all the decisive movements in history are made by minorities, and the Puritans carried with them irresistible elements of strength. They knew exactly what they wanted; their polity was formulated and their discipline worked out.

The conception of a Bible commonwealth was clear to them. And to achieve the ends of this commonwealth, they had entered into a covenant with God and with one another. "We must be knit together in this work as one man, we must entertain each other in brotherly affection." They were embarked upon a mission: "We shall be as a city upon a hill, the eyes of

John Winthrop, 12 times governor of Massachusetts Bay, believed in a Bible commonwealth presided over by an elect minority.

all people are upon us." If they failed, God would make them "a story and a byword through the world, we shall open the mouths of enemies to speak evil of the ways of God and all professors for God's sake." If they succeeded, men would say of later settlements, "The Lord make it like that of New England." We recognize thus early the sense of mission that is so strong in the American make-up today. That came from the Bay Puritans, not from the Plymouth Pilgrims.

The cornerstone of all their churches was a covenant. We find it clearly stated by one of their mentors, the Elizabethan Henry Jacob, a generation before: "A free mutual consent of believers joining and covenanting to live as members of a holy society together in all religious and virtuous duties as Christ and his apostles did institute and practice."

It was this covenant that made them Congregationalists. The Pilgrims at Plymouth were rather a different case, though it seems to be questioned today whether they were absolutely Separatists, wishing to be regarded as utterly separated from the Church of England. They trace their ancestry to the Scrooby congregation, and its pastors and mentors, John Smyth, Richard Clyfton, John Robinson, Elder Brewster. As for the vastly more important Massachusetts Puritans, they held themselves to be Puritan congregations of the Church of England and regarded separation as a sin. They were out to set a better model, and by their example to convert the church at home.

As the *Talbot* drew away from Land's End in 1629—a part of the Puritans' first plantation fleet, the largest that had ever set sail for New England—Francis Higginson spoke these words to the passengers: "We will not say, as the Separatists were wont to say at their leaving of England, 'Farewell, Babylon! Farewell, Rome!' But we *will* say, 'Farewell, dear England! Farewell, the Church of God in England, and all the Christian friends there!' We do not go to New England as Separatists from the Church of England, though we cannot but separate from the corruptions in it, but we go to practice the positive part of Church Reformation, and propagate the Gospel in America."

The Pilgrims were self-effacing exiles who wanted only to escape attention in order to worship and live in their own way; the Massachusetts Puritans were a governing body going forth to convert others.

The 19th century immensely exaggerated the importance of the Pilgrim Fathers. Their story was told in countless books and then put into verse by Longfellow. To judge from its literature, anyone would think that America started with them. It *is* true that the Pilgrims had the advantage of priority, and thereby exerted an influence by the example they set of civil marriage and in the registering of deeds. Theirs also was the first Congregational church, a working model already in be-

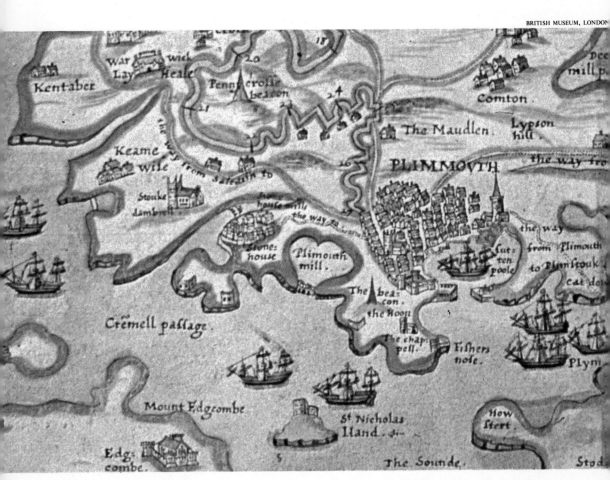

It was from Plymouth harbor, shown on this 1591 map with many surrounding towns, that the Pilgrims finally sailed on the Mayflower *for the New World on September 6, 1620.*

ing when the Massachusetts Puritans began to arrive. But in every other respect the influence was all the other way. The size, power, and importance of the Bay Colony began to tell, until ultimately it absorbed Plymouth.

The religion, and thereby the mentality, of New England was entirely English in its sources. The Scrooby flock had settled in Leyden, where John Robinson was publicly ordained as their pastor; William Brewster became their ruling elder. Prior to emigration, it was agreed that if a majority of the congregation volunteered, Robinson should go as their pastor. To his disappointment, only a minority volunteered. Only 37 of the 100 or more passengers on board the *Mayflower* were Pilgrims from Leyden; we do not know who the rest were, but some of them, we learn from William Bradford, were "profane fellows."

Robinson remained behind to minister to the majority. Meanwhile, he refused to sanction the administration of the sacraments by Elder Brewster in Plymouth. Not being ordained, Brewster might preach and pray, but not give communion. Robinson kept hoping he might be able to join them; he sent them spiritual advice, but soon he was dead. The state of the Pilgrims at Plymouth may be described as "Waiting for Robinson."

However, they got on well without him. Brewster, a mature man of 53 when they landed at Plymouth, had been at Peterhouse, Cambridge, where he acquired nonconforming ideas. He was postmaster in Scrooby, and a pillar of the congregation till 1608. The Scrooby flock left England because it was an ungodly land and found Amsterdam and, subsequently, Leyden uncongenial. Only the wilderness would do, and to the wilderness they went.

Social life in Plymouth has been described as "undoubtedly quiet in the extreme"; but Brewster, according to Bradford, was "of a very cheerful spirit, very sociable and pleasant amongst his friends." He had an excellent library—mostly theology, since he had to preach thrice a week. The rest was mainly practical—herbals, books of surveying and medicine, works on the culture of silkworms

and varieties of timber. In addition were these worldly authors—Machiavelli's *Prince,* Bodin's *Republic,* Bacon's *Advancement of Learning,* and Raleigh's *Prerogatives of Parliaments in England.*

For company there was Miles Standish, Edward Winslow, and Governor Bradford, to whom Elder Brewster stood second in the little colony. Miles Standish was born about 1584, of a younger branch of an old Lancashire family. A professional soldier, he joined the Pilgrims as such, for in religion he was never one of them. He was given command of parties exploring the country and defending the colony against suspect Indians, on one occasion being responsible for a deed of blood against some Indian chiefs. In 1621, he was made captain of the colony, and was often an assistant to the governor. Next to Standish in dealing with the Indians was Winslow, also a man of good family who had joined the Leyden community. Above all, there was Governor Bradford. It is impossible to overestimate what the Plymouth Colony owed to him, for he was, like John Winthrop of the Bay Colony, ideally suited to govern. Bradford brought with him the same Elizabethan ideas on authority that Winthrop had: The main body of the people share in government "only in some weighty matters, when we think good." Queen Elizabeth might have subscribed to that.

As a youth affected by the preaching of Richard Clyfton, William Bradford joined the Scrooby flock and went with Robinson to Leyden. He disliked sectarian labels and wished to retain fellowship with all reformed churches, believing it "great arrogancy for any man or church to think that he or they have so sounded the word of God to the bottom." He was reelected governor 30 times—almost continuously, in fact—in spite of the fear of the New England colonies of a governor for life, and it is obvious that the Pilgrims could not get on without him. His long rule was really one of a benevolent autocracy.

Though not a university man, Bradford was well read, and an excellent historian. His *History of Plymouth Plantation* is considered a masterpiece. In his well-stocked library he, too, had Bodin, Guicciardini's *History of*

Florence, and Peter Martyr's *Decades of the New World.* This Pilgrim governor, so wise, so sober, so restrained—an "achieved spirit," as his age would say—also owned a red waistcoat with silver buttons, a colored hat, and a violet cloak. But it is by his *History* that he lives. It has the qualities that give enduring life to a book—absolute fidelity, lifelikeness, and trustworthiness. Its moral purity—the selflessness, submission, and control—shines through.

For the Elizabethan background of Massachusetts we could not do better than look at the life lived in Groton in the years before John Winthrop left for America. In 1616, Winthrop began a record of his spiritual state, from which we gain an authentic picture of a Puritan's inner mind. John Winthrop felt he was not yet "resolved upon the denial of this world and myself." After his second wife's death he thought he "had brought under my rebellious flesh and prettily tamed it by moderate and spare diet and holding it somewhat close to its task, by prayer, reading, meditation, and the works of my calling." Nevertheless, when he tried to settle down to his ordinary tasks, he found that "the flesh had gotten head and heart again and began to linger after the world; the society of the saints seemed a contemptible thing, meditations were few, prayer was tedious, and fain would the flesh have been at an end before I began." Once more he put himself on a spare diet and set himself to reading devout books. After some time at this, he was surprised to find that he "grew very melancholic and uncomfortable," especially since he had refrained from any "outward conversation in the world." In this condition he began to enjoy experiences like those of St. John of the Cross and St. Theresa. He had such "a heavenly meditation of the love between Christ and me as ravished my heart with unspeakable joy; methought my soul had as familiar and sensible society with him as my wife could have with the kindest husband. I desired no other happiness but to be embraced of him." And, shortly, he was: "O my Lord, my love, how wholly delectable art thou! Let him kiss me with the kisses of his mouth, for his love is sweeter than wine; how

lovely is thy countenance! How pleasant are thy embracings!" This state of exaltation seems to have ended with his third marriage—and perhaps it was about time—in 1618, when his spiritual diary comes to an end. Winthrop got away from this morbid introspection; his impulses found normal channels of expression. He was able to turn to a legal career, becoming an attorney in the Court of Wards and a member of the Inner Temple. External considerations made him decide to go to America; the king's decision to dispense with Parliament meant there was no future for Puritans.

Those who met at Cambridge in August, 1629, and entered into an agreement to go included Thomas Dudley, Sir Richard Saltonstall, William Pynchon, Increase Nowell, and William Vassall. All were Elizabethans. Dudley, born at Northampton in 1576, was the son of a captain "slain in the wars." He enjoyed the ministrations of the Reverend John Cotton and kept in close touch with all the discussions preparatory to the move. He sailed on the *Arbella*—a more important ship than the *Mayflower,* for she carried Winthrop and the Massachusetts leadership on board. Although he was Winthrop's deputy governor, Dudley had a violent quarrel with him over the decision to move from their first site to Boston. They exchanged some ungodly, though not necessarily unpuritanical, words. The two men were hardly congenial. Dudley was dogmatic and overbearing; he had none of Winthrop's moderation, judgment, charm. A man of 54 when he landed in New England, Dudley was tough physically; he produced progeny at the age of 70. He was four times elected governor, 13 times deputy governor; he was one of the first overseers of Harvard, one of the two Massachusetts commissioners who formed the New England Confederation. He was something of a scholar and, like most Elizabethans, wrote verse. A last poem, found in his pocket after his death, spoke his mind on toleration:

Let men of God in courts and churches watch
O'er such as do a toleration *hatch.*

These lines were not without application to such as Saltonstall. Nephew to Sir Richard

The Pilgrims, shown walking to church, worshiped every Sunday from 8 to 12 in the morning and then would meet again in the late afternoon for another long service.

*From left: John Cotton, the Bay Colony's great preacher; Richard Saltonstall, noble-
man and Puritan; Josiah Winslow, founder of the first public school in Massachusetts.*

Saltonstall, who had been lord mayor of London, he was one of the Puritan governing class
who went over on the *Arbella*. But he did not
see eye-to-eye with the rigid exclusiveness of
the theocracy, and was twice fined for back-
sliding in regard to church matters. He returned home next year and never went back.

Pynchon, Nowell, Vassall—all three had
trouble with the ruling authorities. Pynchon,
who helped found Roxbury and Springfield,
wrote a book in 1650 controverting the Cal-
vinist view of the Atonement. When the General Court ordered the book burned, he "decided to return to England, where he might
enjoy that liberty of opinion which was denied
him in the colony he had helped to found."

In 1633, the two authoritative religious
leaders of the first generation, John Cotton and Thomas Hooker, came over. They had
been invited together, but it was wisely decided
that "a couple of such great men might be
more serviceable asunder than together."
Samuel Stone accompanied them, so it was
possible to say, in the punning manner of the
time, that in Massachusetts they now had
"Cotton for their clothing, Hooker for their
fishing, and Stone for their building."

Cotton was probably the leading nonconforming clergyman in the Church of England,
if it is not paradoxical to say so. He became

vicar of the English Boston, where he began
to simplify the services in the interest of more
preaching. He was a great preacher. He soon
developed a faithful following. Like Winthrop,
Cotton was a leader, and this was given full
scope in Massachusetts, where, Roger Williams said, there were people who "could
hardly believe that God would suffer Mr.
Cotton to err."

Cotton and Winthrop were both Elizabethans in their point of view—men whose
minds were geared to government. Cotton's
chief works were in defense of the civil power's
right to interfere in support of the truth, but
he had no more illusions than Winthrop about
the people's fitness to govern. "Democracy,"
he wrote, "I do not conceive that ever God did
ordain as a fit government either for church or
commonwealth." Nevertheless, there was in
Protestantism an inner dynamic that led on to
democracy, and this shortly became evident.

Thomas Hooker, the son of a Leicester-
shire yeoman, was a student at Queen's
College, Cambridge, and became, like Cotton,
a fellow of Emmanuel. At Esher, in Surrey, his
patron's wife believed she had committed the
unpardonable sin—whatever that was. Hooker
succeeded in comforting her, where others
failed. He had a way with him—to the soul.
He married the lady's waiting woman—the

176

proper social status for a clergyman's bride.

Hooker and Stone were called as pastor and teacher of Newton. But they and their congregation became restive under the self-sufficient autocracy of Massachusetts. Hooker's sermon at the making of the Connecticut constitution used to be thought a democratic declaration, for he stated that the "foundation of all authority is the free consent of the people." But we recognize in that the traditional social-contract doctrine as the base of society. "They who have the power to appoint officers and magistrates," he wrote, "it is in their power also to set the bounds and limitations of the power and place unto which they call them." We recognize in that the heart of American political conviction.

The bent of Hooker's mind was, however, evangelical. His books bear such titles as *The Soul's Preparation for Christ, The Soul's Vocation,* and *The Soul's Implantation.* From Con-

necticut, Hooker was called to take part in the controversies that raged in Massachusetts over the tiresome Roger Williams. No sooner had Williams landed in Massachusetts than he discovered that he was "once more in a land where the nonconforming were unfree." He responded by declaring that civil governments had no right to enforce religious injunctions, and when the civil authorities showed they had the power, he took refuge in Plymouth. Later, banished from Massachusetts, he founded a settlement in Providence, the beginning of Rhode Island. Imperial Massachusetts sought to invade Rhode Island and extinguish it; only an appeal to Old England secured a patent and freedom for it to exist.

The Puritans went out to set a model of a godly commonwealth for the world to see and follow. They suffered the fate of all who make an egoistic assumption as to the

On January 21, 1621, the Pilgrims came ashore and held their first religious services on American soil in the newly completed Common House, the first Plymouth building.

course history will take: The course it takes is never what they suppose. Nevertheless, the heroic effort, the sacrifice, had not been in vain. The legacy of the Elizabethan Puritans to New England, though different from what they expected, was a matter of the highest importance. It did not turn out to be New Jerusalem, but it turned out to provide the strongest of bonds to bind together a continental society of a new sort. Something strong, even astringent, was needed to hold together so vast a country; the New England mentality, when it lost the narrowness of its early beliefs, retained a distinguishing element—strongly ethical, seeing life in terms of obligation and duty rather than pleasure. Although the theology and the metaphysics had broken down, the Puritan character remained—the strongest factor in survival. In history, to survive is what matters.

The overwhelmingly theological complexion of the intellectual culture of New England reflected not so much Elizabethan England as Elizabethan Puritanism. But we must not underrate its intellectual energy. Samuel Eliot Morison tells us that "the dominant Puritan clergy, far from being indifferent to culture, did everything possible to stimulate, promote, and even produce intellectual activity. Moreover, it was largely the clergy who persuaded a poor and struggling people to set up schools and a college which continued to serve the community in later centuries."

Their handicaps in keeping civilized standards going were tremendous; theirs was a pioneer country strenuously engaged in the struggle for existence. Yet within 10 years of its founding, Massachusetts had a vigorous intellectual life of its own. No other English commonwealth attempted to provide for learning so soon after it was founded. But New England had Elizabethan England behind it, with its enthusiasm for education, fortified by the Puritan belief in intellect. New Englanders proved their beliefs not only in their precepts but in their works: They were ready to tax themselves for things that in Old England were provided by endowment.

These were the things of the mind, and their minds were formed by the English universities, especially by Cambridge, from which most of the leaders came. There was an average of one university man to every 40 or 50 families—much higher than in Old England. Morison tells us that Puritanism "preserved far more of the humanist tradition than did non-Puritanism in other English colonies." It devoted more attention to classical scholarship and therefore had an interest in making verses, such as all English students were taught to write. So, too, with literary form and style. Morison points out that "the older founders of New England grew up in the age of Shakespeare and the King James Bible," and in consequence these men "wrote prose superior by any standard to that of the later, native-born writers."

However, Shakespeare was precisely what the New England Puritans excluded. They would have suppressed the Elizabethan drama if they could. They had no appreciation of the majesty of the Roman Catholic Church, the Rome of Sixtus V, the music of Palestrina. They had nothing but dislike for the grave and ordered beauty of the Anglican Church, the cadences of the Book of Common Prayer.

The Puritan attitude involved in some ways a denial of life. It was antagonistic to the glorification of the natural man, with all his instincts and appetites, that characterized the Renaissance and the great Elizabethans.

On the other hand, some contraction of response, some repression, produces greater strength and energy with which to face the harsh, sad conditions of pioneer life. And for the life of their community, in probity and public spirit, in moral responsibility and uprightness, in humaneness as to punishment and in mutual help in need, in simple godliness—whether we believe or no, regarding it as a human fact—they *did* exemplify higher standards than any other English society. And theirs more than any others' was the making of the nation.

A. L. Rowse, a fellow of All Souls College, Oxford, and the British Academy, is the author of The Elizabethans in America, The England of Elizabeth, *and many other books.*

FOR FURTHER READING

CHAPTER 4

Boorstin, Daniel J. *The Americans: The Colonial Experience.* New York: Random House, 1958. A general history of the American colonies.

Craven, Wesley F. *The Southern Colonies in the Seventeenth Century, 1607–1689.* Baton Rouge: Louisiana State University Press, 1949. The early history of the Southern colonies examined in detail.

Miller, Perry. *The New England Mind: From Colony to Province.* Cambridge: Harvard University Press, 1953. *The New England Mind: The Seventeenth Century.* New York: Macmillan, 1939. Two books by a leading authority on early New England.

Morgan, E. S. *The Puritan Dilemma: The Story of John Winthrop.* Boston: Little, Brown, 1958. A study of an outstanding Puritan leader.

Morison, Samuel Eliot. *Builders of the Bay Colony.* Boston: Houghton Mifflin, 1930. A scholarly discussion of the founders of the Massachusetts Bay Colony.

Wertenbaker, Thomas J. *The Puritan Oligarchy: The Founding of American Civilization.* New York: Scribner, 1947. An examination of New England life in the 17th century. *Torch Bearer of the Revolution.* Princeton: Princeton University Press, 1940. A study of Nathaniel Bacon that provides a good picture of life in early Virginia.

CHAPTER 5

Ambler, Charles H. *George Washington and the West.* Chapel Hill: University of North Carolina Press, 1936. The personal experiences of Washington as a young man and as an officer in the French and Indian Wars.

Parkman, Francis. *The Battle for North America,* abridged and edited by John Tebbel. Garden City: Doubleday, 1948. A famous historian writes of the French in Canada and their part in the French and Indian Wars.

Van Doren, Carl. *Benjamin Franklin.* New York: Viking, 1938. A Pulitzer Prize winner, it is the standard biography of Franklin.

CHAPTER 6

Becker, Carl L. *The Eve of the Revolution.* New Haven: Yale University Press, 1918. A brief, clear-cut study of the events leading to the Revolution.

Gipson, L. H. *The Coming of the Revolution: 1765–1775.* New York: Harpers, 1954. An important work on the background of the Revolution.

Miller, J. C. *Origins of the American Revolution.* Boston: Little, Brown, 1943. Comprehensive and well written.

Morgan, Edmund S. *The Birth of the Republic: 1763–89.* Chicago: University of Chicago Press, 1956. An interesting and brief account of the onset of the Revolution.

Morris, Richard B., editor. *The Era of the American Revolution.* New York: Columbia University Press, 1939. A useful, varied collection of essays on the Revolution and the events that preceded it.

Rossiter, Clinton. *The First American Revolution.* New York: Harcourt, Brace, 1956. *Seed Time of the Republic.* New York: Harcourt, Brace, 1953. Two books that discuss the background of the Revolution, by a scholarly and imaginative writer.

Savelle, Max. *Seeds of Liberty.* New York: Knopf, 1948. On the intellectual and cultural growth within the colonies.

Wertenbaker, Thomas J. *The Founding of American Civilization* 3 volumes. New York: Scribner, 1938–47. Another study of the intellectual and cultural life in the colonies.

THE AMERICAN HERITAGE NEW ILLUSTRATED HISTORY OF THE UNITED STATES

PUBLISHED BY DELL PUBLISHING CO., INC.

George T. Delacorte, Jr., *Publisher*   Helen Meyer, *President*
William F. Callahan, Jr., *Executive Vice-President*

Walter B. J. Mitchell, Jr., *Project Director;* Ross Claiborne, *Editorial Consultant;* William O'Gorman, *Editorial Assistant;* John Van Zwienen, *Art Consultant;* Rosalie Barrow, *Production Manager*

CREATED AND DESIGNED BY THE EDITORS OF AMERICAN HERITAGE MAGAZINE

James Parton, *Publisher;* Joseph J. Thorndike, Jr., *Editorial Director;* Bruce Catton, *Senior Editor;*
Oliver Jensen, *Editor;* Richard M. Ketchum, *Editor, Book Division;* Irwin Glusker, *Art Director*

ROBERT R. ENDICOTT, *Project Editor-in-Chief*

James Kraft, *Assistant Editor;* Nina Page, Evelyn H. Register, Lynn Marett, *Editorial Assistants;*
Lina Mainiero, *Copy Editor;* Murray Belsky, *Art Director;* Eleanor A. Dye, *Designer;* John Conley, *Assistant*